WHERE WAS GEORGE WASHINGTON?

by Carla Heymsfeld

Illustrations by Jennifer Koury

Published Through the Efforts of

The Founders,

Washington Committee for Historic Mount Vernon

The Mount Vernon Ladies' Association

Mount Vernon, Virginia

1992

Third printing 2014

Copyright 1992 by
The Mount Vernon Ladies' Association
Mount Vernon, Virginia
All rights reserved.
Printed in the United States of America

Library of Congress Cataloging-in-Publication Data

Heymsfeld, Carla.
Where was George Washington? / by Carla Heymsfeld;
illustrations by Jennifer Koury.
p. cm.
"Published through the efforts of The Founders,
Washington Committee for Historic Mount Vernon."
Summary: Describes the daily activities at Mount Vernon in October 1785 and the
work of French artist Jean Antoine Houdon as he prepares to make a statue of
George Washington—as seen through the eyes of a pet cat.
ISBN 0-931917-20-4: $14.95 — ISBN 0-931917-21-2 (pbk.)
1. Washington, George, 1732-1799—Homes and haunts—Virginia—Mount
Vernon (Estate)—Juvenile literature.
2. Washington, George, 1732-1799—Statues—Juvenile literature.
3. Mount Vernon (Va.: Estate)—Juvenile literature.
[1. Mount Vernon (Va.: Estate) 2. Washington, George, 1732-1799—Homes and
haunts. 3. Washington, George, 1732-1799—Statues.]
I. Koury, Jennifer, 1963-   ill.
II. Mount Vernon Ladies' Association of the Union.
III. The Founders, Washington Committee for Historic Mount Vernon.
IV. Title.
E312.5.H64   1992
973.4'1'092—dc20   92-17341
CIP
AC

Designed by Cindy Jackson

WHERE WAS
GEORGE WASHINGTON?

Liberty's whiskers twitched as she looked around George Washington's study. It was a beautiful October morning in 1785 and Liberty was ready to start her day.

Where could General Washington be?

Every day as soon as the General got up, he came downstairs to dress and do his work. And every day when Liberty came along to meow a good morning, he was there to scratch behind her ears.

But not today.

Perhaps he was at breakfast. Liberty padded into the small dining room and jumped onto George Washington's chair. Dirty dishes and leftover food were all that remained of the morning meal. Corn crumbs floating in honey and butter told her that the General had eaten his usual mush cakes, and extra places at the table told her he'd had company for breakfast.

Grabbing a fat herring, she carried her prize to a comfortable spot on the floor. She nibbled happily until her sharp ears heard the footsteps of Frank Lee, the butler, coming to clear the table.

It was time to move on.

Then Liberty remembered the new roof. The other day, General Washington had watched his carpenters from the courtyard as they put up shingles and coppered the gutters. Maybe they hadn't finished.

Tail high, she walked outside to investigate. The scaffold was gone. The shingles and gutters were in place.

The only people in the courtyard were Nelly Custis, Mrs. Washington's six-year-old granddaughter, and Nelly's younger brother, Washy. They were standing in front of the kitchen house peeking in the door.

Liberty joined them.

She saw Herculus, one of the cooks, rolling dough for currant tarts. She heard the crackle of the roaring fire and smelled fish chowder bubbling in the big black kettle.

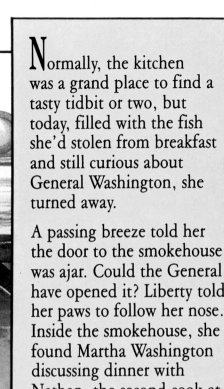

Normally, the kitchen was a grand place to find a tasty tidbit or two, but today, filled with the fish she'd stolen from breakfast and still curious about General Washington, she turned away.

A passing breeze told her the door to the smokehouse was ajar. Could the General have opened it? Liberty told her paws to follow her nose. Inside the smokehouse, she found Martha Washington discussing dinner with Nathan, the second cook at Mount Vernon. When they agreed on a large ham, Liberty knew there would be company for dinner, too. She watched with interest as Nathan began climbing the ladder to reach the meat.

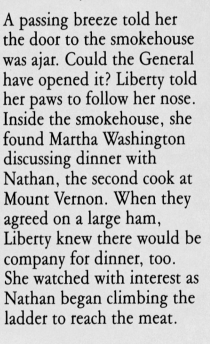

All of a sudden,
the ladder toppled.

DOWN CAME NATHAN.

DOWN CAME THE HAM.

*DOWN CAME THE DUCKS
AND THE FISH.*

This was no time to
linger in the smokehouse.

Liberty darted through the door and continued her   search for Ge

shington

In the stable yard, Joe, the coachman, was washing the carriage. It had been splattered with mud on Sunday when the family rode home from church. Pohick Church was 10 miles away on dirt roads, and the carriage often needed a bath after the trip.

Liberty did not want to get in Joe's way, not while he had a big pail of water so handy. She would look for George Washington somewhere else. Circling around the coach-house she entered the wash yard.

Dolly and Sall Brass, the two washerwomen who did the laundry for the family and their guests, were working very hard.

A basket filled with clean clothes sat on the grass next to Dolly. What a comfortable spot! Liberty put her two front paws on the edge. The basket tipped.

"YOU BAD CAT!" Dolly called, as Liberty dragged a petticoat through a muddy puddle.

Backing out of the petticoat, Liberty ran until she reached the old cowpen George Washington was turning into a bowling green. She stepped carefully through the freshly seeded field and entered the courtyard again. Strange voices were speaking a foreign language. Fascinated by the musical words, Liberty followed the sounds until she came to the servants' hall.

There was George Washington, but *OH MY!* He was stretched out on a long table and covered with a sheet.

Four men were painting white plaster all over his face. Two breathing straws poked through to his nose.

Liberty heard a small scream behind her. *"GRANDPAPA!"* Nelly Custis cried. *"WHAT IS THE MATTER WITH GRANDPAPA?*

IS HE DEAD?"

"No, no, little mademoiselle. Do not worry yourself," one of the men said. "It is only a plaster mask on your grandpapa's face."

"A mask? For what?" Nelly asked.

The man smiled. "Monsieur Jean Antoine Houdon is a famous sculptor from France. He is making a statue of your grandfather. The mask will help him shape the face."

George Washington raised a hand and waved it in Nelly's direction. She ran to him and held it tightly.

Soon Mr. Houdon removed the mask. George Washington sat up and wiped his face with a warm, wet towel.

"See?" he said to Nelly as they examined the mask. "There is the shape of my face, only inside out. If we poured plaster into it and let it dry, the hardened plaster would come out looking like me."

Liberty could not see inside the mask, but she was curious. Some plaster had dropped on the floor and she touched it lightly. Nothing happened. She would have to be bolder. Putting her paw firmly on the lump of plaster, she pressed harder. This time she felt the plaster give. Liberty pulled out her foot and looked proudly at the inside-out image of her paw.

While Liberty was admiring her paw print, Mr. Houdon and his assistants did something else to help them remember George Washington. They measured him. They measured his height, they measured his arms, they measured his legs. They measured his waist, they measured his neck and they measured his fingers. They measured his nose and his upper lip. The statue was going to stand in the Virginia State Capitol building in Richmond so Mr. Houdon wanted it to be exactly right.

After a while, George Washington stretched and said, "That's enough for this morning. Nelly, let's go see if Herculus left apples near the stable. We'll give Nelson a treat."

Nelly clapped her hands. "Blueskin, too?" she begged.

"Blueskin, too." Her grandfather laughed.

Liberty ran ahead. She liked Nelson and Blueskin, George Washington's old war horses. Retired now, they lived quietly in the new brick stable at the end of the south lane.

Liberty jumped on the wall of Blueskin's stall, surprising him with a loud meow. Blueskin started, knocking Liberty from her perch. The frightened cat tumbled over his back and onto the floor. Darting past Blueskin's sharp hooves, Liberty escaped to the paddock.

Blueskin, upset by the excitement, was not far behind.

From the safety of the paddock fence, Liberty watched Mr. Houdon and his assistants talk among themselves and make notes in a little book. She wondered why they were there. Washy must have wondered, too, because he asked his grandfather what they were doing.

"They're watching me," George Washington explained. "My statue will be more like me if they see how I move, what I do with my hands, and what my face looks like when I talk to people."

"Do you mind?" Nelly asked.

"I try to forget about them," her grandfather answered.

The next day everyone gathered to see the bust Mr. Houdon made of George Washington. Liberty looked at the clay head and shoulders and thought they looked just right, but Mr. Houdon wasn't satisfied. He added a bit of clay here and he removed a bit of clay there. Finally he was ready to put it in the oven.

"Baking will make it hard," George Washington explained.

They all trooped across the courtyard to the kitchen, even Liberty. Mr. Houdon put the bust in the oven. In a little while it was done.

Mr. Houdon used the hard clay bust to make a mold. With the mold he could make more heads. Liberty watched Mr. Houdon pour plaster into the mold. He let it harden. When he opened it up, there was the head of George Washington! Liberty was impressed.

When Mr. Houdon finished his work and was ready to leave Mount Vernon, Liberty watched the sculptor and his assistants carefully load all their crates onto George Washington's barge, which would take them down the Potomac River to the port of Alexandria. From there, the assistants would sail back to France, while Mr. Houdon would head for Philadelphia to show off his new work of art.

Liberty was sorry to see them go, but was pleased that they left the original clay bust behind as a gift for George Washington.

Every day after Mr. Houdon left, Liberty went into General Washington's study to look at the clay bust. Four years later, when George Washington became president and did not live at Mount Vernon, the bust was a great comfort to her.

Whenever she was lonely she would stretch out on the floor under the familiar clay face. It wasn't the same as having the real George Washington at home, but it looked so much like him that she could pretend.

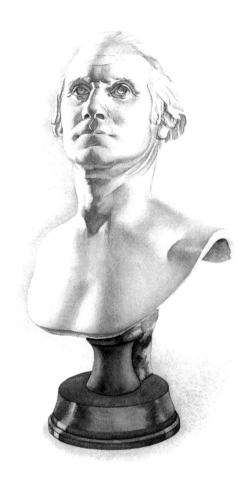

Today, when you visit Mount Vernon, you can see this clay bust in the museum on the estate. If you do, you will know just how George Washington looked, even though he lived 200 years ago.

NOTES ON HISTORY

The people, places, and events in *Where Was George Washington?* are true to history. During the years between the end of the American Revolution and his election as our first president, George Washington returned to Mount Vernon. Jean Antoine Houdon came to the plantation in October of 1785 to make a bust of him. When six-year-old Nelly saw him stretched out in the servants' hall, she really was afraid he was dead. We know this from a letter she wrote to her brother many years later.

Washington's diaries tell us that the roof of the west front of the mansion was shingled at this time and that the cowpen was plowed up and grass seed was planted to create a bowling green.

All the rooms and buildings are described and drawn to reflect their 18th-century appearance and use. The people mentioned in the story really existed. Nelly and Washy lived at Mount Vernon and the pictures of them in the book are based on their portraits.

As for Liberty, well. . . we don't know if she ever existed, but we like to think maybe she did.

Mount Vernon, the home of George Washington, is America's oldest national historic preservation project. The estate is owned and operated by the Mount Vernon Ladies' Association, which has restored and protected the estate since 1858 without funding from the federal government, relying solely on admission fees and private contributions. All proceeds from the sale of this book will be used to preserve and maintain this historic treasure for future generations.